A DAY OF PLEASANT BREAD

BY
DAVID GRAYSON

ILLUSTRATED BY
THOMAS J. FOGARTY

RENAISSANCE
HOUSE PUBLISHERS

541 Oak Street • P.O. Box 177
Frederick, CO 80530

ISBN: 1-55838-098-1

RENAISSANCE HOUSE PUBLISHERS
A Division of Jende-Hagan, Inc.
541 Oak Street ~ P.O. Box 177
Frederick, CO   80530

A DAY OF PLEASANT BREAD
is excerpted from the book-length
ADVENTURES IN FRIENDSHIP,
Renaissance House, 1989

A DAY OF
PLEASANT BREAD

A DAY OF PLEASANT BREAD

THEY have all gone now, and the house is very still. For the first time this evening I can hear the familiar sound of the December wind blustering about the house, complaining at closed doorways, asking questions at the shutters; but here in my room, under the green reading lamp, it is warm and still. Although Harriet has closed the doors, covered the coals in the fireplace, and said good-night, the atmosphere still seems to tingle with the electricity of genial humanity.

The parting voice of the Scotch Preacher still booms in my ears:

"This," said he, as he was going out of our door, wrapped like an Arctic highlander in cloaks and tippets, "has been a day of pleasant bread."

One of the very pleasantest I can remember!

I sometimes think we expect too much of Christmas Day. We try to crowd into it the long arrears of kindliness and humanity of the whole year. As for me, I like to take my Christmas a little at a time, all through the year. And thus I drift along into the holidays—let them overtake me unexpectedly —waking up some fine morning and suddenly saying to myself:

"Why, this is Christmas Day!"

How the discovery makes one bound out of his bed! What a new sense of life and adventure it imparts! Almost anything may happen on a day like this—one thinks. I may meet friends I have not seen before in years. Who knows? I may discover that this is a far better and kindlier world than I had ever dreamed it could be.

So I sing out to Harriet as I go down:

"Merry Christmas, Harriet"—and not

"MERRY CHRISTMAS, HARRIET"

waiting for her sleepy reply I go down and build the biggest, warmest, friendliest fire of the year. Then I get into my thick coat and mittens and open the back door. All around the sill, deep on the step, and all about the yard lies the drifted snow: it has transformed my wood pile into a grotesque Indian mound, and it frosts the roof of my barn like a wedding cake. I go at it lustily with my wooden shovel, clearing out a pathway to the gate.

Cold, too; one of the coldest mornings we've had—but clear and very still. The sun is just coming up over the hill near Horace's farm. From Horace's chimney the white wood-smoke of an early fire rises straight upward, all golden with sunshine, into the measureless blue of the sky—on its way to heaven, for aught I know. When I reach the gate my blood is racing warmly in my veins. I straighten my back, thrust my shovel into the snow pile, and shout at the top of my voice, for I can no longer contain myself:

"Merry Christmas, Harriet."

Harriet opens the door—just a crack.

"Merry Christmas yourself, you Arctic explorer! Oo—but it's cold!"

And she closes the door.

Upon hearing these riotous sounds the barnyard suddenly awakens. I hear my horse whinnying from the barn, the chickens begin to crow and cackle, and such a grunting and squealing as the pigs set up from behind the straw stack, it would do a man's heart good to hear!

"It's a friendly world," I say to myself, "and full of business."

I plow through the snow to the stable door. I scuff and stamp the snow away and pull it open with difficulty. A cloud of steam arises out of the warmth within. I step inside. My horse raises his head above the stanchion, looks around at me, and strikes his forefoot on the stable floor—the best greeting he has at his command for a fine Christmas morning. My cow, until now silent, begins to bawl.

I lay my hand on the horse's flank and he steps over in his stall to let me go by. I slap his neck and he lays back his ears playfully. Thus I go out into the passageway and give my horse his oats, throw corn and stalks to the pigs and a handful of grain to Harriet's chickens (it's the only way to stop the cackling!). And thus presently the barnyard is quiet again except for the sound of contented feeding.

Take my word for it, this is one of the pleasant moments of life. I stand and look long at my barnyard family. I observe with satisfaction how plump they are and how well they are bearing the winter. Then I look up at my mountainous straw stack with its capping of snow, and my corn crib with the yellow ears visible through the slats, and my barn with its mow full of hay —all the gatherings of the year, now being expended in growth. I cannot at all explain it, but at such moments the circuit of that dim spiritual battery which each of us conceals within seems to close, and the full current of contentment flows through our lives.

All the morning as I went about my chores I had a peculiar sense of expected pleasure. It seemed certain to me that something unusual and adventurous was about to happen—and if it did not happen offhand, why I was there to make it happen! When I went in to breakfast (do you know the fragrance of broiling bacon when you have worked for an hour before breakfast on a morning of zero weather? If you do not, consider that heaven still has gifts in store for you!)—when I went in to breakfast, I fancied that Harriet looked preoccupied, but I was too busy just then (hot corn muffins) to make an inquiry, and I knew by experience that the best solvent of secrecy is patience.

"David," said Harriet, presently, "the cousins can't come!"

"Can't come!" I exclaimed.

"Why, you act as if you were delighted."

"No—well, yes," I said, "I knew that some extraordinary adventure was about to happen!"

"Adventure! It's a cruel disappointment —I was all ready for them."

"Harriet," I said, "adventure is just what we make it. And aren't we to have the Scotch Preacher and his wife?"

"But I've got such a *good* dinner."

"Well," I said, "there are no two ways about it: it must be eaten! You may depend upon me to do my duty."

"We'll have to send out into the highways and compel them to come in," said Harriet ruefully.

I had several choice observations I should

have liked to make upon this problem, but Harriet was plainly not listening; she sat with her eyes fixed reflectively on the coffee-pot. I watched her for a moment, then I remarked:

"There aren't any."

"David," she exclaimed, "how did you know what I was thinking about?"

"I merely wanted to show you," I said, "that my genius is not properly appreciated in my own household. You thought of highways, didn't you? Then you thought of the poor; especially the poor on Christmas day; then of Mrs. Heney, who isn't poor any more, having married John Daniels; and then I said, 'There aren't any.'"

Harriet laughed.

"It has come to a pretty pass," she said, "when there are no poor people to invite to dinner on Christmas day."

"It's a tragedy, I'll admit," I said, "but let's be logical about it."

"I am willing," said Harriet, "to be as logical as you like."

"Then," I said, "having no poor to invite to dinner we must necessarily try the rich. That's logical, isn't it?"

"Who?" asked Harriet, which is just like a woman. Whenever you get a good healthy argument started with her, she will suddenly short-circuit it, and want to know if you mean Mr. Smith, or Joe Perkins's boys, which I maintain is *not* logical.

"Well, there are the Starkweathers," I said.

"David!"

"They're rich, aren't they?"

"Yes, but you know how they live—what dinners they have—and besides, they probably have a houseful of company."

"Weren't you telling me the other day how many people who were really suffering were too proud to let anyone know about it? Weren't you advising the necessity of getting acquainted with people and finding out—tactfully, of course—you made a point of tact—what the trouble was?"

"But I was talking of *poor* people."

"Why shouldn't a rule that is good for poor people be equally as good for rich people? Aren't they proud?"

"Oh, you can argue," observed Harriet.

"And I can act, too," I said. "I am now going over to invite the Starkweathers. I heard a rumor that their cook has left them and I expect to find them starving in their parlour. Of course they'll be very haughty and proud, but I'll be tactful, and when I go away I'll casually leave a diamond tiara in the front hall."

"What *is* the matter with you this morning?"

"Christmas," I said.

I can't tell how pleased I was with the enterprise I had in mind: it suggested all sorts of amusing and surprising developments. Moreover, I left Harriet, finally, in the breeziest of spirits, having quite forgotten her disappointment over the non-arrival of the cousins.

"If you *should* get the Starkweathers——"

" 'In the bright lexicon of youth,' " I observed, " 'there is no such word as fail.' "

So I set off up the town road. A team or two had already been that way and had broken a track through the snow. The sun was now fully up, but the air still tingled with the electricity of zero weather. And the fields! I have seen the fields of June and the fields of October, but I think I never saw our countryside, hills and valleys, tree

spaces and brook bottoms, more enchant-
ingly beautiful than it was this morning.
Snow everywhere—the fences half hidden,
the bridges clogged, the trees laden: where
the road was hard it squeaked under my feet,
and where it was soft I strode through the
drifts. And the air went to one's head like
wine!

So I tramped past the Pattersons'. The old
man, a grumpy old fellow, was going to the
barn with a pail on his arm.

"Merry Christmas," I shouted.

He looked around at me wonderingly and
did not reply. At the corners I met the
Newton boys so wrapped in tippets that
I could see only their eyes and the red ends of
their small noses. I passed the Williams's
house, where there was a cheerful smoke in
the chimney and in the window a green wreath
with a lively red bow. And I thought how
happy everyone must be on a Christmas morning like this! At the hill bridge who should
I meet but the Scotch Preacher himself, God
bless him!

"Well, well, David," he exclaimed heartily,
"Merry Christmas."

I drew my face down and said solemnly:

"Dr. McAlway, I am on a most serious errand."

"Why, now, what's the matter?" He was all sympathy at once.

"I am out in the highways trying to compel the poor of this neighbourhood to come to our feast."

The Scotch Preacher observed me with a twinkle in his eye.

"David," he said, putting his hand to his mouth as if to speak in my ear, "there is a poor man you will na' have to compel."

"Oh, you don't count," I said. "You're coming anyhow."

Then I told him of the errand with our millionaire friends, into the spirit of which he entered with the greatest zest. He was full of advice and much excited lest I fail to do a thoroughly competent job. For a moment I think he wanted to take the whole thing out of my hands.

"Man, man, it's a lovely thing to do," he exclaimed, "but I ha' me doots—I ha' me doots."

At parting he hesitated a moment, and with a serious face inquired:

"Is it by any chance a goose?"

"It is," I said, "a goose—a big one."

He heaved a sigh of complete satisfaction. "You have comforted my mind," he said, "with the joys of anticipation—a goose, a big goose."

So I left him and went onward toward the Starkweathers'. Presently I saw the great house standing among its wintry trees. There was smoke in the chimney but no other evidence of life. At the gate my spirits, which had been of the best all the morning, began to fail me. Though Harriet and I were well enough acquainted with the Starkweathers, yet at this late moment on Christmas morning it did seem rather a hair-brained scheme to think of inviting them to dinner.

"Never mind," I said, "they'll not be displeased to see me anyway."

I waited in the reception-room, which was cold and felt damp. In the parlour beyond I could see the innumerable things of beauty—furniture, pictures, books, so very, very much of everything—with which the room was filled. I saw it now, as I had often seen it before, with a peculiar sense of weariness. How all these things, though beautiful enough in themselves, must clutter up a man's life!

Do you know, the more I look into life, the more things it seems to me I can successfully lack—and continue to grow happier. How many kinds of food I do not need, nor cooks to cook them, how much curious clothing nor tailors to make it, how many books that I never read, and pictures that are not worth while! The farther I run, the more I feel like casting aside all such impedimenta—lest I fail to arrive at the far goal of my endeavour.

I like to think of an old Japanese nobleman I once read about, who ornamented his house with a single vase at a time, living with it, absorbing its message of beauty, and when he tired of it, replacing it with another. I wonder if he had the right way, and we, with so many objects to hang on our walls, place on our shelves, drape on our chairs, and spread on our floors, have mistaken our course and placed our hearts upon the multiplicity rather than the quality of our possessions!

Presently Mr. Starkweather appeared in the doorway. He wore a velvet smoking-jacket and slippers; and somehow, for a bright morning like this, he seemed old, and worn, and cold.

"Well, well, friend," he said, "I'm glad to see you."

He said it as though he meant it.

"Come into the library; it's the only room in the whole house that is comfortably warm. You've no idea what a task it is to heat a place like this in really cold weather. No sooner do I find a man who can run my furnace than he goes off and leaves me."

"I can sympathize with you," I said, "we often have trouble at our house with the man who builds the fires."

He looked around at me quizzically.

"He lies too long in bed in the morning," I said.

By this time we had arrived at the library, where a bright fire was burning in the grate. It was a fine big room, with dark oak furnishings and books in cases along one wall, but this morning it had a dishevelled and untidy look. On a little table at one side of the fireplace were the remains of a breakfast; at the other a number of wraps were thrown carelessly upon a chair. As I came in Mrs. Starkweather rose from her place, drawing a silk scarf around her shoulders. She is a robust, rather handsome woman, with many rings on her fingers, and a pair of glasses hanging to a little gold hook on her ample bosom; but this morning she, too, looked worried and old.

"Oh, yes," she said with a rueful laugh, "we're beginning a merry Christmas, as you see. Think of Christmas with no cook in the house!"

I felt as if I had discovered a gold mine. Poor starving millionaires!

But Mrs. Starkweather had not told the whole of her sorrowful story.

"We had a company of friends invited for dinner to-day," she said, "and our cook was ill—or said she was—and had to go. One of the maids went with her. The man who looks after the furnace disappeared on Friday, and the stableman has been drinking. We can't very well leave the place without some one who is responsible in charge of it—and so here we are. Merry Christmas!"

I couldn't help laughing. Poor people!

"You might," I said, "apply for Mrs. Heney's place."

"Who is Mrs. Heney?" asked Mrs. Starkweather.

"You don't mean to say that you never heard of Mrs. Heney!" I exclaimed. "Mrs. Heney, who is now Mrs. 'Penny' Daniels? You've missed one of our greatest celebrities."

With that, of course, I had to tell them about Mrs. Heney, who has for years performed a most important function in this community. Alone and unaided she has been the poor whom we are supposed to have always with us. If it had not been for the devoted faithfulness of Mrs. Heney at Thanksgiving, Christmas and other times of the year, I suppose our Woman's Aid Society and the King's Daughters would have perished miserably of undistributed turkeys and tufted comforters. For years Mrs. Heney filled the place most acceptably. Curbing the natural outpourings of a rather jovial soul she could upon occasion look as deserving of charity as any person that ever I met. But I pitied the little Heneys: it always comes hard on the children. For weeks after every Thanksgiving and Christmas they always wore a painfully stuffed and suffocated look. I only came to appreciate fully what a self-sacrificing public servant Mrs. Heney really was when I learned that she had taken the desperate alternative of marrying "Penny" Daniels.

"So you think we might possibly aspire to the position?" laughed Mrs. Starkweather.

Upon this I told them of the trouble in our household and asked them to come down and help us enjoy Dr. McAlway and the goose.

When I left, after much more pleasant talk, they both came with me to the door seeming greatly improved in spirits.

"You've given us something to live for, Mr. Grayson," said Mrs. Starkweather.

So I walked homeward in the highest spirits, and an hour or more later who should we see in the top of our upper field but Mr. Starkweather and his wife floundering in the snow. They reached the lane literally covered from top to toe with snow and both of them ruddy with the cold.

"We walked over," said Mrs. Starkweather breathlessly, "and I haven't had so much fun in years."

Mr. Starkweather helped her over the fence. The Scotch Preacher stood on the steps to receive them, and we all went in together.

I can't pretend to describe Harriet's dinner: the gorgeous brown goose, and the apple sauce, and all the other things that best go with it, and the pumpkin pie at the end —the finest, thickest, most delicious pumpkin pie I ever ate in all my life. It melted in one's mouth and brought visions of celestial bliss. And I wish I could have a picture of Harriet presiding. I have never seen her happier, or more in her element. Every time she brought in a new dish or took off a cover it was a sort of miracle. And her coffee—but I must not and dare not elaborate.

And what great talk we had afterward!

I've known the Scotch Preacher for a long time, but I never saw him in quite such a mood of hilarity. He and Mr. Starkweather told stories of their boyhood—and we laughed, and laughed—Mrs. Starkweather the most of all. Seeing her so often in her carriage, or in the dignity of her home, I didn't think she had so much jollity in her. Finally she discovered Harriet's cabinet organ, and nothing would do but she must sing for us.

"None of the new-fangled ones, Clara," cried her husband: "some of the old ones we used to know."

So she sat herself down at the organ and threw her head back and began to sing:

"Believe me, if all those endearing young charms,
    Which I gaze on so fondly to-day——,"

Mr. Starkweather jumped up and ran over to the organ and joined in with his deep voice. Harriet and I followed. The Scotch Preacher's wife nodded in time with the music, and presently I saw the tears in her eyes. As for Dr. McAlway, he sat on the edge of his chair with his hands on his knees and wagged his shaggy head, and before we got through he, too, joined in with his big sonorous voice:

"Thou wouldst still be adored as this moment thou
    art——,"

Oh, I can't tell here—it grows late and there's work to-morrow—all the things we did and said. They stayed until it was dark, and when Mrs. Starkweather was ready to go, she took both of Harriet's hands in hers and said with great earnestness:

"I haven't had such a good time at Christmas since I was a little girl. I shall never forget it."

And the dear old Scotch Preacher, when Harriet and I had wrapped him up, went out, saying:

"This has been a day of pleasant bread."

It has; it has. I shall not soon forget it. What a lot of kindness and common human nature—childlike simplicity, if you will—there is in people once you get them down together and persuade them that the things they think serious are not serious at all.

David Grayson was the pen name of accomplished turn-of-the-century journalist Ray Stannard Baker. Baker had a long, productive relationship with the prestigious *McClure's* magazine, bringing to its pages portraits of some of the day's geniuses: Theodore Roosevelt, Joel Chandler Harris, Stephen Crane, Admiral Dewey, Thomas A. Edison, Guglielmo Marconi. At a political gathering in January, 1910, he was enlightened by a speech from the president of Princeton University. Thus began the close friendship of Ray Stannard Baker and Woodrow Wilson, Baker following the future President throughout his administration and ultimately to Europe in 1918. He organized the press department at the Paris Peace Conference and reported the long, often bitter controversies over the League of Nations. Baker became Woodrow Wilson's official biographer and was awarded the Pulitzer Prize for his seven-volume *Woodrow Wilson: Life and Letters.*

But Ray Stannard Baker was a lover of quiet ways and simple pleasures: goals not easily attained in the hectic journalistic world. Thus emerged David Grayson, the writer in Baker who "wished most, if it can be expressed in a phrase, to be an introducer of human beings to one another, to be a maker of understandings." In pursuit of a more rational lifestyle, he moved his family to Amherst, Massachusetts, where they built their quiet, country dream home. From this refuge, Grayson recorded his daily thoughts and observations on the state of the farm, his neighbors, his bees, the nation and mankind.